How To Win At
TABLE TENNIS

(FOR LOSERS)

Lard Cake Productions
copyright © LCP

STOP.....BEING.....A.....LOSER.

STOP....

BEING.....

A.....

LOSER.

STOP.....

BEING.....

A....

LOSER.

STOP.....

BEING.....

A.....

LOSER.

STOP.....

BEING.....

A.....

LOSER.

STOP.....

BEING.....

A.....

LOSER.

STOP.....

BEING.....

A.....

,

LOSER.

STOP.....

BEING.....

A.....

LOSER.

STOP.....

BEING.....

A.....

LOSER.

STOP.....

BEING.....

A.....

LOSER.

STOP.....

BEING.....

A.....

LOSER.

STOP.....

BEING.....

A.....

LOSER.

STOP.....

BEING.....

A......

LOSER.

STOP.....

BEING.....

A.....

LOSER.

STOP.....

BEING.....

A.....

LOSER.

STOP.....

BEING.....

A.....

LOSER.

STOP.....

BEING.....

A.....

LOSER.

STOP.....

BEING.....

A.....

LOSER.

STOP.....

BEING.....

A.....

LOSER.

STOP.....

BEING.....

A.....

LOSER.

STOP.....

BEING.....

A.....

LOSER.

STOP.....

BEING.....

A.....

LOSER.

STOP.....

BEING.....

A.....

LOSER.

STOP.....

BEING.....

A.....

LOSER.

STOP.....

BEING.....

A.....

LOSER.

STOP.....

BEING.....

A.....

LOSER.

STOP.....

BEING.....

A....

LOSER.

STOP.....

BEING.....

A....

LOSER.

STOP.....

BEING.....

A....

LOSER.

STOP.....

BEING.....

A....

LOSER.

STOP.....

BEING.....

A....

LOSER.

STOP.....

BEING.....

A....

LOSER.

STOP.....

BEING.....

A....

LOSER.

STOP.....

BEING.....

A....

LOSER.

STOP.....

BEING.....

A....

LOSER.

NOW YOU ARE READY.

GO WIN!

Made in the USA
Monee, IL
20 December 2020